WHEN DISASTER STRIKES

EXTREME EARTHQUAKES

AND TSUNAMIS

Thanks to the creative team:

Senior Editor: Alice Peebles
Fact checking: Tom Jackson
Illustration: Jeremy Pyke
Picture Research: Nic Dean
Design: www.collaborate.agency

First published in Great Britain in 2017
by Hungry Tomato Ltd
PO Box 181
Edenbridge
Kent, TN8 9DP

A CIP catalogue record for this book is
available from the British Library.

ISBN 978-1-912108-71-8

Printed and bound in China

Discover more at
www.hungrytomato.com

WHEN DISASTER STRIKES
EXTREME EARTHQUAKES AND TSUNAMIS

by John Farndon

HUNGRY
TOMATO™

CONTENTS

Earthquakes and Tsunamis   6

How Does an Earthquake Happen?   8

Earthquake Damage   10

After an Extreme Earthquake   12

Extreme Earthquake Story   14

One Step Ahead of the Earthquake   16

How Does a Tsunami Happen?   18

Extreme Tsunami Damage   20

Extreme Tsunami Story   22

One Step Ahead of the Tsunami   24

Intense Futures   26

Timeline   28

Blown Away!   30

Index   32

EARTHQUAKES

Earthquakes are a violent shaking of the ground. They are set off by a sudden snapping or shifting of the giant slabs of rock that make up the Earth's surface. Most are so faint that they are only detectable on the most sensitive equipment. But a few are so powerful they can cause devastation, destroying cities and killing many people.

TSUNAMIS

A tsunami is a wave, or series of waves, set off when an earthquake or volcanic eruption under the sea moves a lot of water. The movement spreads out in all directions. While under the sea, it cannot be seen, but once it reaches the coast it sends up huge walls of water that can cause devastation, washing away everything in its path.

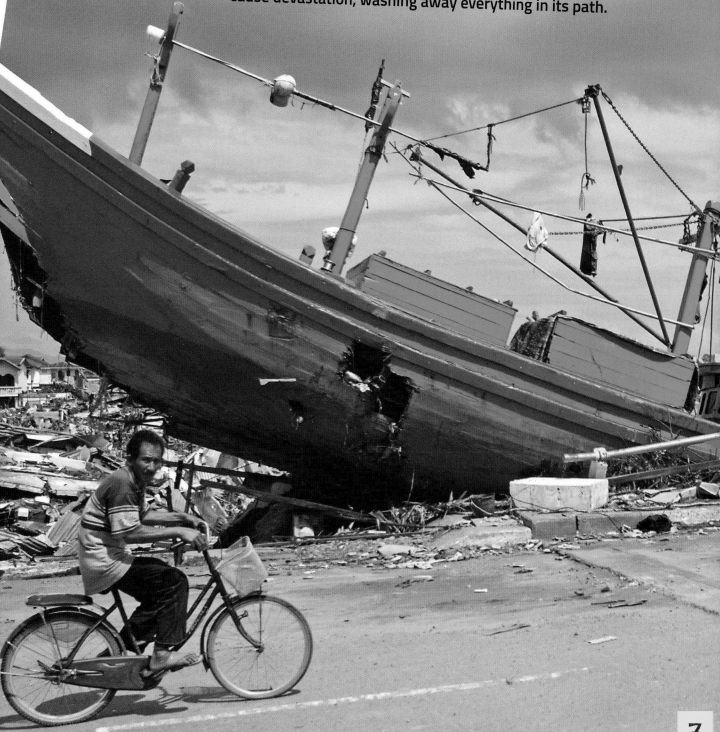

HOW DOES AN EARTHQUAKE HAPPEN?

The Earth's solid surface, or crust, is cracked into giant slabs of rock called tectonic plates. These slabs are always grinding past each other. Most earthquakes happen when two slabs suddenly crack or slip. As they slip, they send out shock waves or 'seismic waves' through the ground.

UNBELIEVABLE!

There is no chance of running away from an earthquake. The fastest earthquake waves roar through the ground at 8 km/sec (5 mps) – that's over 40 times as fast as a jet airliner!

CALIFORNIA ALERT

The San Andreas fault zone in California is a transform (see right) over 1,300 km (800 miles) long. Here the tectonic plate under the Pacific Ocean grinds past the North American plate. Movement along this fault frequently causes earthquakes, such as the quake that devastated San Francisco in 1906. Experts believe it will cause another massive one in the future.

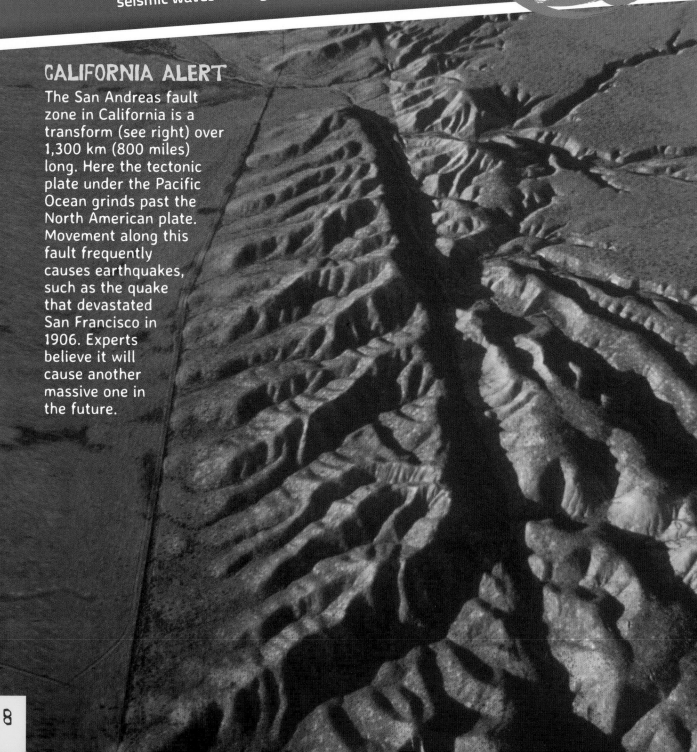

SHAKING PLATES

Some tectonic plates pull apart, some push together, and some slide sideways past each other. It is these sliding junctions, known as 'transforms', that set off most earthquakes. The jagged edges of the plates snag together, allowing pressure to build up, until they suddenly slip, setting off an earthquake.

Some plates pull away from each other (rifts)

Some plates slide sideways past each other (transforms)

Some plates push on top of another (subduction)

UNDERWATER VOLCANO

Most earthquakes are set off by tectonic plates juddering past each other. But a few may be set off by volcanoes. As the hot magma pushes into cracks in the rock under a volcano, it can make the rock snap and send out an earthquake.

QUAKE ZONES

Nowhere in the world is completely immune from earthquakes. Yet most big earthquakes occur in belts or 'earthquake zones' along the boundaries between tectonic plates. Around 80 per cent of all big quakes strike around the edge of the Pacific Ocean, while many of the rest rumble through southern Europe, the Near East and southern Asia.

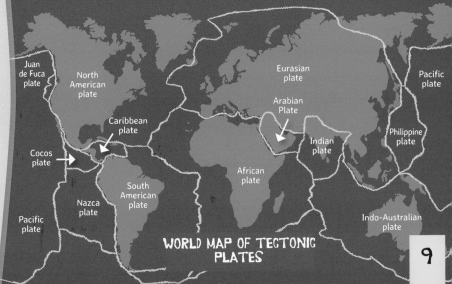

Juan de Fuca plate
North American plate
Eurasian plate
Pacific plate
Arabian Plate
Caribbean plate
Indian plate
Philippine plate
Cocos plate
African plate
South American plate
Nazca plate
Pacific plate
Indo-Australian plate

WORLD MAP OF TECTONIC PLATES

9

EARTHQUAKE DAMAGE

When an earthquake hits, it shakes the ground violently to and fro. At the epicentre of a powerful shallow quake, the shaking is so severe that even the strongest buildings may not survive. It can also open up giant cracks, and throw the ground sideways or up or down, or start avalanches. It can also turn the ground almost to liquid.

UNBELIEVABLE!
In 2010, an earthquake in Chile moved the city of Concepción 3 m (10 ft) to the west. The quake also shortened Earth's day fractionally!

HAITI TRAGEDY
The quake that hit the island republic of Haiti and its capital Port-au-Prince (main picture) on 12 January 2010 had a terrible effect. The poorly built houses collapsed, over 160,000 people died, and three million had their homes ruined. Disruption of water supplies led to a horrible outbreak of the disease cholera.

FIRE DAMAGE
Some of the worst earthquake damage is caused by fire, often set off by damage to gas pipes and electrical cables. When a huge earthquake hit San Francisco on 18 April 1906, it was one of the worst natural disasters in US history. But most of the damage was done by the fires that raged for three days after the quake.

DEADLY SURPRISE

One of the worst aspects of earthquakes is that they can strike out of the blue. Even in an earthquake zone, centuries can go by with no disturbance. That's what happened in the historic town of Amatrice in Italy. Then with no warning, in August 2016, the town was utterly destroyed by a quake in just a few minutes.

BROKEN BRIDGE

Bridges are very vulnerable to quakes. Just a tiny movement can snap a span, with devastating consequences. So engineers in quake zones build bridges such as the San Francisco Bay Bridge, to be as earthquake-resistant as possible.

AFTER AN EXTREME EARTHQUAKE

Few earthquakes last for more than a minute. But in that brief time, they can do terrible damage. The sooner the emergency services can move in to help, the better. But with roads broken, water and power supplies cut off, and buildings in danger of further collapse, they have a very challenging task.

UNBELIEVABLE!

A massive $3.5 billion was raised by ordinary people worldwide to help victims of the 2010 Haiti earthquake. Some movie stars donated $1 million each, while Brazilian model Gisele Bundchen gave $1.5 million and Tiger Woods $3 million.

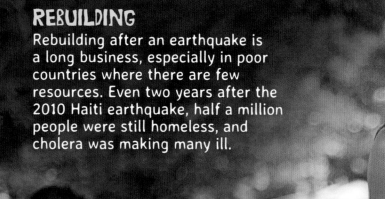

REBUILDING

Rebuilding after an earthquake is a long business, especially in poor countries where there are few resources. Even two years after the 2010 Haiti earthquake, half a million people were still homeless, and cholera was making many ill.

DETECTION EQUIPMENT

Modern technology can be a great help in finding survivors. Video cameras can be squeezed through holes on narrow poles. Thermal imagers can pick up body heat in dark places. And specialist sound equipment can pick up the sounds of breathing — but rescuers have to be very quiet themselves.

RESCUE DOGS

One of the first tasks is to rescue survivors still trapped under collapsed buildings. To help find them, rescuers may use sniffer dogs whose keen sense of smell enables them to pick up on signs of life that human rescuers cannot. The dogs can also work over a large area quickly.

OUTSIDE HELP

Victims of earthquakes need help not only with rescue efforts but rebuilding afterwards. Disaster relief workers, rescue teams, medical staff, technicians and security personnel may be sent to help at once. And ordinary people around the world may raise money to buy everything from fresh water to new furniture.

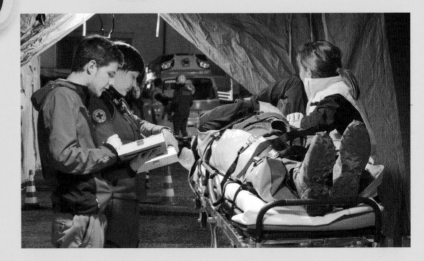

MEDICAL AID

Doctors and nurses are vital in the aftermath of a quake, not only for treating terrible injuries. Illnesses may set in as food and water supplies are disrupted. Water often gets polluted by dirt and sewage, causing cholera, dysentery and other water-borne diseases.

EXTREME EARTHQUAKE STORY

The earthquake that hit the town of Valdivia in Chile on 22 May 1960 was the most powerful ever recorded. It began 160 km (100 miles) offshore at 15.11 pm and shook Valdivia and towns along the coast almost instantly. But it was the giant tsunami that hit the shore 15 minutes later that did most of the damage.

UNBELIEVABLE!
A quarter of all the earthquake energy of the 20th century, including the 2004 Indian Ocean quake, was concentrated in the 1960 Chile quake.

HOW BIG?

Scientists use devices called seismometers to register an earthquake's vibrations or waves. In the past, they rated their size on a scale, called the Richter scale, from 0 to over 9, the strongest. But for the biggest earthquakes, they now use the Moment Magnitude scale. This combines Richter readings with observations of rock movements to show the true power of an earthquake.

Plate movement

Plate movement

Seismic waves

Focus

POWER QUAKES

The Valdivia quake was 9.4–9.6 on the Moment Magnitude scale. Only six other quakes have ever been above 9.

22 May 1960	Valdivia, Chile	9.4–9.6
27 March 1964	Prince William Sound, Alaska	9.2
26 December 2004	Sumatra, Indonesia	9.1–9.3
11 March 2011	Tohoku region, Japan	9.1[4]
4 November 1952	Kamchatka, USSR	9.0
13 August 1868	Arica, Chile (then Peru)	9.0
26 January 1700	Cascadia, Pacific Ocean	8.7–9.2

1960 Valdivia Earthquake

Japan

North America

20

15

South America

10

Australia

5

◎ Epicentre   Travel time (in hours) of wave front

BIG IN JAPAN

Earthquakes as big as Valdivia send their effects worldwide. The tremors from Valdivia could be detected on seismometers on the other side of the world. And the tsunami unleashed travelled right across the Pacific Ocean to Japan in just 22 hours, causing a devastating 5.5-m (18-ft) wave.

DOWN UNDER

Many earthquakes start when tectonic plates slide sideways past each other. The Valdivia quake was different. It started under the sea in a deep ocean trench off the Chilean coast. Here, one plate is 'subducted' or thrust underneath the neighbouring plate. The quake started when the western edge of the South American plate lurched 18 m (60 ft) up over the Nazca plate near the base of the trench.

Subducted area ruptures, releasing energy in an earthquake

15

ONE STEP AHEAD OF THE EARTHQUAKE

Many large cities – such as Los Angeles, Mexico City and Tokyo – are located in areas prone to earthquakes. Sooner or later, one will be hit by a 'Big One'. So the more warning people get, the better. Scientists know why quakes happen, but it is hard to predict when they will.

UNBELIEVABLE!

Do animals know quakes are coming? In 1975, scientists in Yingkou in China noticed snakes and rats emerging from their holes. The city was evacuated just before a huge quake struck, and many lives were saved.

AN EYE ON THE WORLD

Earthquake monitoring stations around the world are now linked together to keep a constant eye on earthquake activity. The Global Seismographic Network (GSN) keeps over 150 stations linked via the internet to quickly detect and pinpoint every significant earthquake anywhere.

TESTING THE GROUND

Many seismologists believe the answer is to watch for signs of strain building up in the rocks. In many earthquake zones, high precision surveys now monitor the ground for any signs of deformation in the rocks. Accurate surveys on the surface, for instance, may pick up slight horizontal movements, while tiltmeters set underground may show any vertical shift

EARLY WARNING

The waves that do most damage in a quake are called S-waves. But waves called P-waves travel much faster and arrive first. In Japan, if a network of monitoring stations detects the P-waves from an approaching quake, they instantly broadcast an alert on TV and radio, and alarms sound in schools and factories.

Fault line

Earthquake sensor

Earthquake alert centre

First P-Wave

Epicentre

More severe S-waves

THE POWER OF AN EARTHQUAKE

The Richter scale, devised in 1935 by earthquake scientist Charles Richter, measures the magnitude (size) of an earthquake. Each step from 1 to 10 on the scale indicates a tenfold increase in energy. The typical effects given for each step may vary widely.

Scale	Damage
0–1.9	Can't be felt by people
2–2.9	Felt by some people, no damage
3–3.9	Visible shaking, occasional damage
4–4.9	Rattling, things fall off shelves
5–5.9	Felt by all, damage to rickety buildings
6–6.9	Violent shaking near epicentre, damage to buildings
7–7.9	Damage or collapse of most buildings, felt 250 km (155 miles) away
8–8.9	Most buildings destroyed near epicentre
9 and over	Total destruction over a large area

HOW DOES A TSUNAMI HAPPEN?

Tsunamis are a brief series of waves like the ripples from a stone thrown in a pond – only much, much bigger! A tsunami typically begins with an earthquake – maybe when a big chunk of the Earth's crust snaps in the seafloor, sending pulses of water through the ocean in all directions.

UNBELIEVABLE

Tsunamis can also be started by the impact of a meteor landing, although this is rare. But geologists have found evidence that 2.2 million years ago, a meteor landed in the Pacific Ocean 1,500 km (930 miles) west of Chile.

HIDDEN TERROR

Out at sea, tsunamis travel unseen along the seabed. But they move faster than a jet airliner. Once they reach shallow water, they may slow down a little, but like water slopping at the edge of a bath, they can rear up to frightening heights.

JAPAN

One or two major tsunamis strike somewhere in the world every year. But Japan gets more than most (Tohoku, March 2011, shown). Tsunami is Japanese for 'harbour wave', so-called because fishermen never saw these waves at sea — then returned home to find their harbour devastated.

An earthquake sends water rolling across the seafloor at high speed

Near the coast, the backwards roll of the tsunami pulls water away from the shore

EYEWITNESS

The first sign of a tsunami may be the sea suddenly receding. When the Boxing Day 2004 tsunami hit the beach at Phuket in Thailand, 10-year-old British tourist Tilly Smith remembered this from a geography lesson and warned people on the beach to run inland in time to save their lives.

The tsunami rears up and rolls right over, crashing on to the shore

TSUNAMI SPEEDS

The deeper the water in which a tsunami travels, the faster it can move. A deep tsunami can travel right across the Pacific Ocean in less than 20 hours!

Depth (m)	Speed (km/h)	Depth (ft)	Speed (mph)
7,000	943	23,000	586
4,000	713	13,000	443
2,000	313	6,500	194
200	159	650	99
50	79	165	49
10	36	33	22

VOLCANIC TSUNAMIS

Not all tsunamis are generated by earthquakes. Some are set off by erupting volcanoes. One of the worst tsunamis ever occurred on 26 August 1883, after the explosion and collapse of the volcano of Krakatoa in Indonesia. It sent out waves reaching 40 m (135 ft), and destroyed coastal towns and villages on Java and Sumatra, killing 36,417 people.

1 Original summit of volcano

4 Lateral blast

5 Debris crashes into the sea

2 Volcano collapses

6 Tsunami forms

3 Magma body is unroofed

EXTREME TSUNAMI DAMAGE

Perhaps no natural disaster is quite so shattering and sudden as a tsunami. It comes suddenly out of the sea with little or no warning to swamp coastlines with giant walls of water that can wash away everything and sweep far inland.

UNBELIEVABLE

One man survived the 1883 Krakatoa tsunami by jumping on the back of a giant crocodile. He held on to it as the wave swept them inland for two miles and crashed on a hill. He then jumped off and ran for his life.

SWEPT TO SHORE

An indication of the amazing power of a tsunami is shown by this engraving made after a tsunami hit Sumatra in Indonesia following the eruption of Krakatoa in 1883. This steamship was travelling calmly out at sea. Minutes later it had been swept a mile inland. Its crew of 28 all died.

EYEWITNESS

As the Tohoku tsunami (right) rolled in, people saw their homes being swept away. One witness heard the cry "Tsunami coming!" almost half a mile inland. "I rushed up the stairs to the rooftop of the building with the residents. The tsunami hit the centre. The building was surrounded by water and wreckage of houses and buildings. The water reached as high as the ceiling of the second floor."

TOHOKU DISASTER

On 11 March 2011, a gigantic earthquake shook the ocean floor 70 km (43 miles) off the east coast of Japan. It set off a tsunami hitting the Sendai region with waves up to 40.5 m (133 ft) tall and roared 10 km (6 miles) inland. A million buildings were destroyed or badly damaged and nearly 16,000 people lost their lives.

Fukushima Daiichi

Tokyo

⊚ Epicentre

◯ Radioactive contamination

⬙ Damaged nuclear power plant

NUCLEAR FEAR

Many of Japan's nuclear power plants are on the coast, in the direct line of tsunamis. The Tohoku tsunami of 2011 caused one of the world's most terrifying nuclear accidents went it hit the Fukushima power plant, destroying the cooling system of one of the reactors. The reactor went into meltdown, triggering fears of a catastrophic leak of radioactive material.

EXTREME TSUNAMI STORY

On 26 December 2004, the seafloor off the coast of Sumatra in south-east Asia was rocked by the second biggest earthquake ever recorded. The earthquake itself did little damage on land, but it ripped apart the seabed and lifted it 15 m (49 ft) along a huge stretch of fault in the Sunda Trench, sending a devastating tsunami across the Indian Ocean.

UNBELIEVABLE

The earthquake that triggered the Boxing Day tsunami was the longest ever – lasting up to 10 minutes. It made the whole Earth wobble up to 2 cm (0.7 in) off its axis.

BANDA ACEH

On the shores directly facing the quake, the tsunami reared up to over 30 m (98 ft) and roared over a mile inland. The nearby Sumatran city of Banda Aceh (main picture) was hit by the full force of the tsunami five minutes after the quake began, and destroyed almost totally in 15 minutes, with tens of thousands people killed.

STRANDED

This boat left perched on top of two houses gives an idea of just how extreme the effect of the tsunami was — and also the problems with clearing up. Just how do you get a boat off the roof and back to the sea?

DISASTER RELIEF

The Boxing Day tsunami was one of the worst natural disasters ever. Besides claiming the lives of about 230,000 people, it left millions homeless. A massive international programme was launched to rescue and aid survivors.

Bangladesh

India
18,045 dead

Myanmar
400–600 dead

Somalia
289 dead

Andaman
Islands

Maldives
108 dead

Sri Lanka
35,322 dead

Thailand
8,212 dead

Malaysia
75 dead

Seychelles
3 dead

INDIAN
OCEAN

Indonesia
167,799 dead

Madagascar

OCEAN WIDE

Within half an hour, the tsunami had swamped the Andaman Islands hundreds of kilometres away, and within an hour and half it had overwhelmed the coastal resorts of Thailand with a wall of water 10 m (30 ft) high. In two hours, the tsunami raced thousands of kilometres across the Indian Ocean to hit Sri Lanka and southern India. Over 100,000 people died in Indonesia, close to the origin, but 289 people died even in Somalia, East Africa.

EMERGENCY AID

After the tsunami, emergency crews rushed into action dropping water, food and medical supplies by helicopter, since many roads were washed away. But the disaster was so widespread, that many people and remote villages received no help at all.

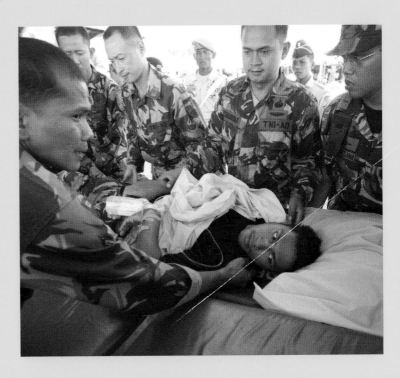

23

ONE STEP AHEAD OF THE TSUNAMI

Tsunamis can take several hours to travel across the ocean. So if scientists can detect a tsunami early on, they may be able to issue warnings and give people a chance to escape. Nowadays, the Pacific Tsunami Warning System goes on to alert every time the Global Seismographic (see p. 16) detects a large, shallow quake under the Pacific Ocean.

UNBELIEVABLE

After the Boxing Day tsunami of 2004, researchers found that much less damage was done where the shoreline was protected by coral reefs or vegetation. Human activity weakens these natural defences through pollution and deforestation, for example.

NOAA — TSUNAMI

TSUNAMI BUOYS

The DART system is a series of 40 or so buoys dotted across the ocean and linked by sound waves to special pressure sensors on the ocean floor. These sensors can detect a slight rise or fall in the depth of water above — even as little as 1 mm (0.03 in). If there is a sudden change, the buoy sends out the alarm via a satellite link.

TSUNAMI WARNING

Japan has a network of more than 300 sensors on the islands and in the sea to monitor changes in water level and quake activity. If a tsunami looks likely, an alert can be sounded in just three minutes with sirens and messages on TV and radio. Now alerts can be sent by text message to everyone with a mobile phone.

DROPPING DARTS

To pick up tsunamis early, the buoys have to be near the places where they start. That means they must be scattered across the ocean floor — particularly near deep trenches in the ocean floor where earthquakes often happen. They are dropped at the right location by helicopters and anchored in place by weighted cables.

SEA DEFENCE

Early warning may help people to evacuate coastal areas before a tsunami strikes, but the impact of tsunamis can also be reduced by natural and artificial barriers on the shore. In the city of Numazu in Japan, they have built a giant gate across the dock entrance. It can be dropped closed in just five minutes to block off a tsunami as much as 6 m (20 ft) high.

INTENSE FUTURES

Scientists have put a lot of effort into trying to work out when and where the next big earthquake or tsunami will strike. The best they can do so far is give us a little warning once it has already begun. But somewhere, somehow in the future a major disaster will happen, we can be sure.

MONSTER WAVE

Cumbre Vieja is a volcano on the Canary Islands in the Atlantic. One day in the future some of it might suddenly collapse into the sea. If so, could it unleash a mega-tsunami which could sweep across the Atlantic? Vast waves hundreds of metres high might crash over the cities of Boston, New York and Miami as in this imaginary picture. Luckily, most scientists think this is unlikely.

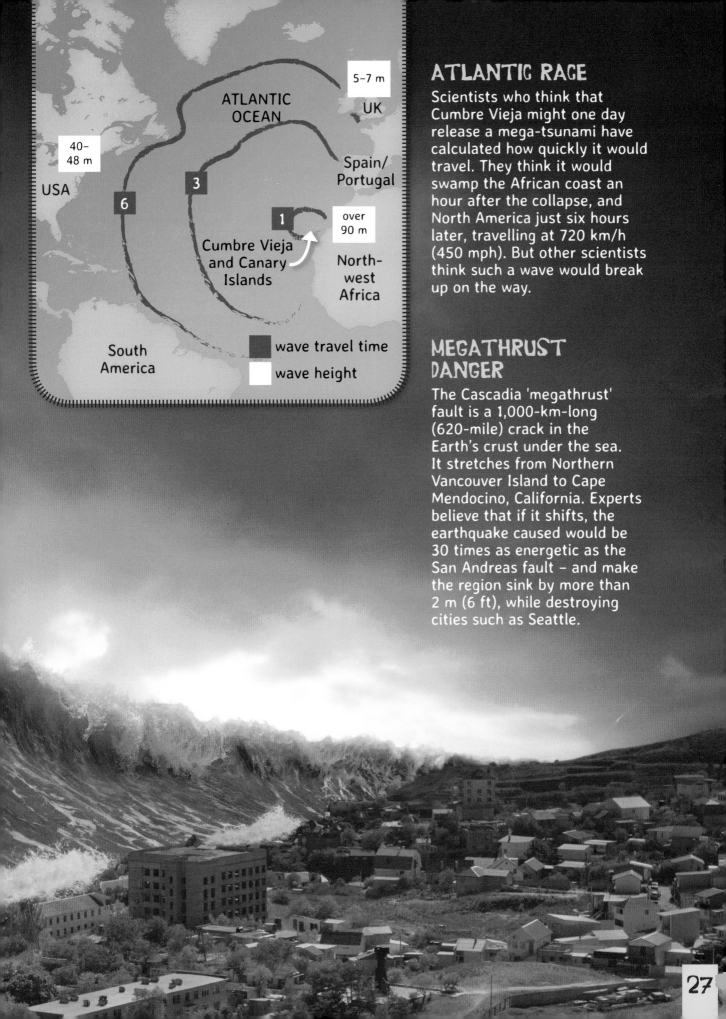

ATLANTIC OCEAN

5–7 m
UK

40–48 m

USA

3

6

1

over 90 m

Cumbre Vieja and Canary Islands

Spain/Portugal

North-west Africa

South America

■ wave travel time
□ wave height

ATLANTIC RACE

Scientists who think that Cumbre Vieja might one day release a mega-tsunami have calculated how quickly it would travel. They think it would swamp the African coast an hour after the collapse, and North America just six hours later, travelling at 720 km/h (450 mph). But other scientists think such a wave would break up on the way.

MEGATHRUST DANGER

The Cascadia 'megathrust' fault is a 1,000-km-long (620-mile) crack in the Earth's crust under the sea. It stretches from Northern Vancouver Island to Cape Mendocino, California. Experts believe that if it shifts, the earthquake caused would be 30 times as energetic as the San Andreas fault – and make the region sink by more than 2 m (6 ft), while destroying cities such as Seattle.

TIMELINE

1906
After the Great San Francisco Earthquake, a firestorm raged and left many homeless

132 CE
Zhang Heng invented the first earthquake detector (replica shown)

1923
Much of Tokyo, Japan, was destroyed in a fire after the Great Kanto Earthquake, killing more than 140,000 people and destroying 360,000 buildings (below)

1054 ●

1775
After an earthquake in Portugal, a huge tsunami hit Lisbon, with waves over 15 m (50 ft) high

1935
American Charles Richter invented the Richter scale to measure earthquake magnitude

1885
British geologist John Milne invented the first modern seismograph

1960
The largest earthquake ever recorded, 9.5 on the Richter scale, hit Chile, creating tsunamis that caused damage as far away as Japan

1556
A massive earthquake hit Shaanxi province in China, killing 830,000 people

2010
A quake hit the city of Port-au-Prince in Haiti, killing 160,000 people, and displacing very many, including this child

1989
The Loma Prieta earthquake in Santa Cruz brought an elevated freeway crashing down and was broadcast live on TV

1988
An earthquake in Armenia brought down newly built apartments, killing 25,000

1999
An earthquake in Turkey killed 17,000 people

● **2011**

1976
An earthquake measuring 7.8 hit Tangshan, China, killing up to 655,000 people

2001
An earthquake in Gujarat, India, killed 20,000 people

2005
A 7.6 earthquake in Pakistan and Kashmir killed over 86,000 people

1995
In Kobe, Japan, 6,400 people died in a 7.2 earthquake

2003
An earthquake in Iran killed 26,000 people and destroyed the ancient city of Bam

1970
An earthquake in Peru set off a massive avalanche in the mountains that killed 18,000 people

2004
A huge earthquake off Sumatra, Indonesia, triggered the Boxing Day tsunami that killed over 230,000 people around the Indian Ocean

2011
The Tohoku earthquake off the east coast of Japan caused terrible tsunamis

29

BLOWN AWAY!

Amazing facts about
earthquakes and tsunamis

LOST TIME

Earthquakes can make the whole Earth move! The 2011 Tohoku quake in Japan shifted the Earth's mass and made the Earth spin faster, shortening the day by 1.6 microseconds. The 2004 Sumatra quake shortened the day by 6.8 microseconds.

BRIGHT SPARKS

Three Greek scientists, professors Varotsos, Alexopoulos and Nomikos, developed a system to predict earthquakes known as the VAN method after their initials. It looks for disturbances in natural electric currents, called telluric currents, flowing in the ground. They managed to predict some quakes this way. But most scientists are not yet convinced by the idea.

MOONQUAKE

The moon has quakes, too – only they are called moonquakes, not earthquakes. They are normally weaker than earthquakes.

A TINY SHIFT

Tectonic plates, those giant slabs of rock that make up the Earth's surface, move very slowly – less than 17 cm (3 in) per year. But a tectonic plate only has to budge 20 cm (8 in) or so to set off a major earthquake.

NOSE FOR A QUAKE

Sometimes, ponds and canals give off a strange smell before an earthquake. Scientist think the smell comes from the release of gases underground. The water on the ground can also become warmer.

Mount Bromo, Indonesia, sits on the Ring of Fire

QUAKES IN 3D

In recent years, earthquake scientists have begun to bring the massive calculating power of supercomputers to bear on predicting earthquakes. The Quake Project at the Southern California Earthquake Centre is working with one of the world's fastest computers to build a 3D computer model of just what goes on in the ground during an earthquake. It uses very detailed seismograph data.

EARTHQUAKE HOTSPOTS

Four of every five big quakes happen around the 'Ring of Fire'. This is a huge ring around the Pacific Ocean where many tectonic plates meet. The second most earthquake-prone area is the Alpide Belt, which spans Turkey, India and Pakistan.

WORST EARTHQUAKES

WORLD'S DEADLIEST
Shaanxi province, China
23 January 1556
Cost in lives: over 830,000

DEADLIEST RECENT
Tangshan, China
27 July 1976
Cost in lives: up to 655,000

MOST POWERFUL
Valdivia, Chile
22 May 1960
Magnitude: 9.4-9.6 on the Richter magnitude scale

MOST EXPENSIVE
Tohoku, Japan
11 March 2011
Cost: $235 billion

MOST POWERFUL IN THE USA
Prince William Sound,
south-central Alaska
27 March 1964
Magnitude: 9.2 on the Richter magnitude scale

WORST TSUNAMIS

WORLD'S DEADLIEST
Crete earthquake tsunami,
Eastern Mediterranean, Greece
21 July 365 CE
Cost in lives: maybe up to 500,000

DEADLIEST RECENT
Boxing Day tsunami, Indian Ocean
26 December 2004
Cost in lives: 280,000

MOST EXPENSIVE
Tohoku tsunami, Japan
11 March 2011
Cost: $235 billion

TALLEST
Lituya Bay tsunami, Alaska
9 July 1958
Height: 524 m (1,720 ft)

FASTEST
Boxing Day tsunami, Indian Ocean
26 December 2004
Speed: 800 km/h (500 mph)

INDEX

A
aftermath of earthquakes 12, 13
aftermath of tsunamis 19, 20, 21, 22, 23
Alaska earthquake 15
Amatrice earthquake 11

B
Boxing Day tsunami 19, 22, 23
bridges 11

C
Cumbre Vieja 26, 27
causes of earthquakes 8, 9, 15
causes of tsunamis 18, 19

D
damage
  earthquakes 10, 11
  tsunamis 20, 21
DART system 24, 25
detection equipment 12
disaster relief 13, 23

E
early detection
  earthquakes 16, 17, 30, 31
  tsunamis 24, 25
earthquake zones 9, 31
emergency aid 13, 23

F
fire damage 10
floods 19, 20, 21, 22, 23
future disasters 26, 27

H
Haiti earthquake 10, 12

K
Krakatoa tsunami 19, 20

M
medical aid 13
Moment Magnitude scale 14, 15

Q
Quake Project 31

R
Richter scale 14, 17
rescue efforts 12, 13, 23

S
San Andreas fault 8
San Francisco earthquake 8, 10
seismometers 14
size of earthquakes 6, 15, 17, 30

T
tectonic plates 8, 9, 15, 30
Tohoku earthquake 6, 15, 30
Tohoku tsunami 21

V
Valdivia earthquake 14, 15
volcanoes 9, 19, 26

W
warning signs and systems 17, 19, 24, 25
water supplies 13
worst earthquakes 31
worst tsunamis 31

THE AUTHOR

John Farndon is Royal Literary Fellow at City&Guilds in London, UK, and the author of a huge number of books for adults and children on science, technology and nature, including such international best-sellers as *Do Not Open* and *Do You Think You're Clever?* He has been shortlisted six times for the Royal Society's Young People's Book Prize for a science book, with titles such as *How the Earth Works, What Happens When?* and *Project Body* (2016).